EUROPE

ASIA

AFRICA

ARABIA

INDIA

PACIFIC OCEAN

INDIAN OCEAN

AUSTRALIA

New Zealand

Cocos Islands

St Helena

Cape Horn

mouth

A N T A R C T I C   O C E A N

What Mr Darwin Saw

For our own little apes:
Max, Bjorn, Frej
and Charlie Manning

Mick and Brita wish to thank the
Natural History Museum and in particular
Judith Magee, Max Barclay and
David M Williams.

JB Darwin G

What Mr Darwin Saw

by Mick Manning and Brita Granström

F

FRANCES LINCOLN
CHILDREN'S BOOKS

In association with the
Natural History Museum, London

Erasmus Darwin, Charles's grandfather, was a doctor, naturalist and poet who was already writing about evolution in the 1790s.

Early Days 1809-1825

I was born on 12 February 1809. My mother died when I was eight years old. By the time I went to school my taste for natural history was well developed. I collected all sorts of things. When I left school I was considered by my father a very ordinary boy. My father once said to me, "You care for nothing but shooting, dogs and rat catching and you will be a disgrace to yourself and your family." But my father was the kindest man I ever knew and must have been angry when he used such words.

It's a big 'un!

As a young lad Charles spent a lot of time hunting rats . . . and shooting snipe.

Blugh!

Edinburgh University 18²⁵-18²⁶

As I was no good at school, my father sent me to Edinburgh University. I attended the operating theatre and saw two very bad operations, but I rushed away before they were completed. Nor did I ever attend again; it disgusted me and the cases haunted me for many a year. After having spent two sessions in Edinburgh, my father heard from my sisters that I did not like the thought of being a physician, so he proposed that I should study to become a clergyman.

Tonight Darwin, we're eating a brown owl!

Cheers!

Yuck!

At Cambridge, Darwin was a member of the Glutton Club. They would meet once a week to eat 'strange meat' like fox, badger and even an owl!

Darwin met a naturalist called Professor Henslow at Cambridge who encouraged his interest in science.

Has anyone seen young Darwin?

Cambridge University 1828 - 1830

During the years which I spent at Cambridge my time was wasted, as completely as at Edinburgh! No pursuit at Cambridge gave me so much pleasure as collecting beetles. One day I saw two rare beetles and seized one in each hand; then I saw a third and new kind, which I could not bear to lose, so that I popped it into my mouth . . . but it squirted some fluid that burnt my tongue and I was forced to spit the beetle out . . .

You may as well fly to the moon!

Charles's father was against his son sailing. But Charles's uncle, Josiah Wedgewood, persuaded him to relent!

You must keep a loaded pistol at all times.

Captain FitzRoy helped Darwin choose a pair of pistols for the dangerous voyage.

Aye-aye shipmates!

I look forward to your company, Mr Darwin.

When do we sail, Captain FitzRoy?

HMS *Beagle* sailed from Portsmouth, England in December 1831.

Our adventure begins Mr Darwin!

FitzRoy was one of the best sea captains of his day with many fresh ideas.

We're almost ship-shape.

The Beagle is ready!

Adventure Begins! Autumn 1831

Returning home from a short geological tour in North Wales I found a letter from Professor Henslow informing me that Captain FitzRoy was willing to give up half of his cabin to any young man that would go along without pay as a gentleman companion on the voyage of HMS *Beagle*. Captain FitzRoy was devoted to his duty; generous to a fault, bold, determined, energetic and a friend. A handsome man with courteous manners. I was instantly eager . . . but my father strongly objected.

FitzRoy's mission was to survey the coastline of South America and take time measurements around the world. Darwin was very seasick.

Setting Sail *December 1831*

I am on board HMS *Beagle*, a fast survey ship armed with cannons. We are in the Bay of Biscay and there is a good deal of swell on the sea. Out of spirits and very sick. I find the only thing my stomach can bear is biscuit and raisins.

Darwin read Charles Lyell's book *Principles of Geology* on the voyage – it opened his mind to many new ideas about how the earth was created.

Crossing the Equator January 1832

We have crossed the equator and I have undergone the disagreeable operation of being shaved by Neptune's constables. They lathered my face with tar and paint! I was blindfolded then placed on a plank which could be tilted up into a bath of water. I was tilted head over heels into the water where two men ducked me!

Darwin marvelled at the leaf-cutter ants. Their trails were everywhere in the forest.

Darwin wondered why a butterfly should have patterns on its wings like owls. Did they help it survive in some way?

Salvador Rainforest *February 1832*

I have been wandering in the Brazilian rainforest! It is hard to say what is most striking: the vegetation, the elegance of the grasses, the novelty of the parasitical plants, the beauty of the flowers . . . A mixture of sound and silence pervades the shady parts of the wood . . . The air is deliciously cool and soft. I collected numberless small beetles and a most beautiful large lizard.

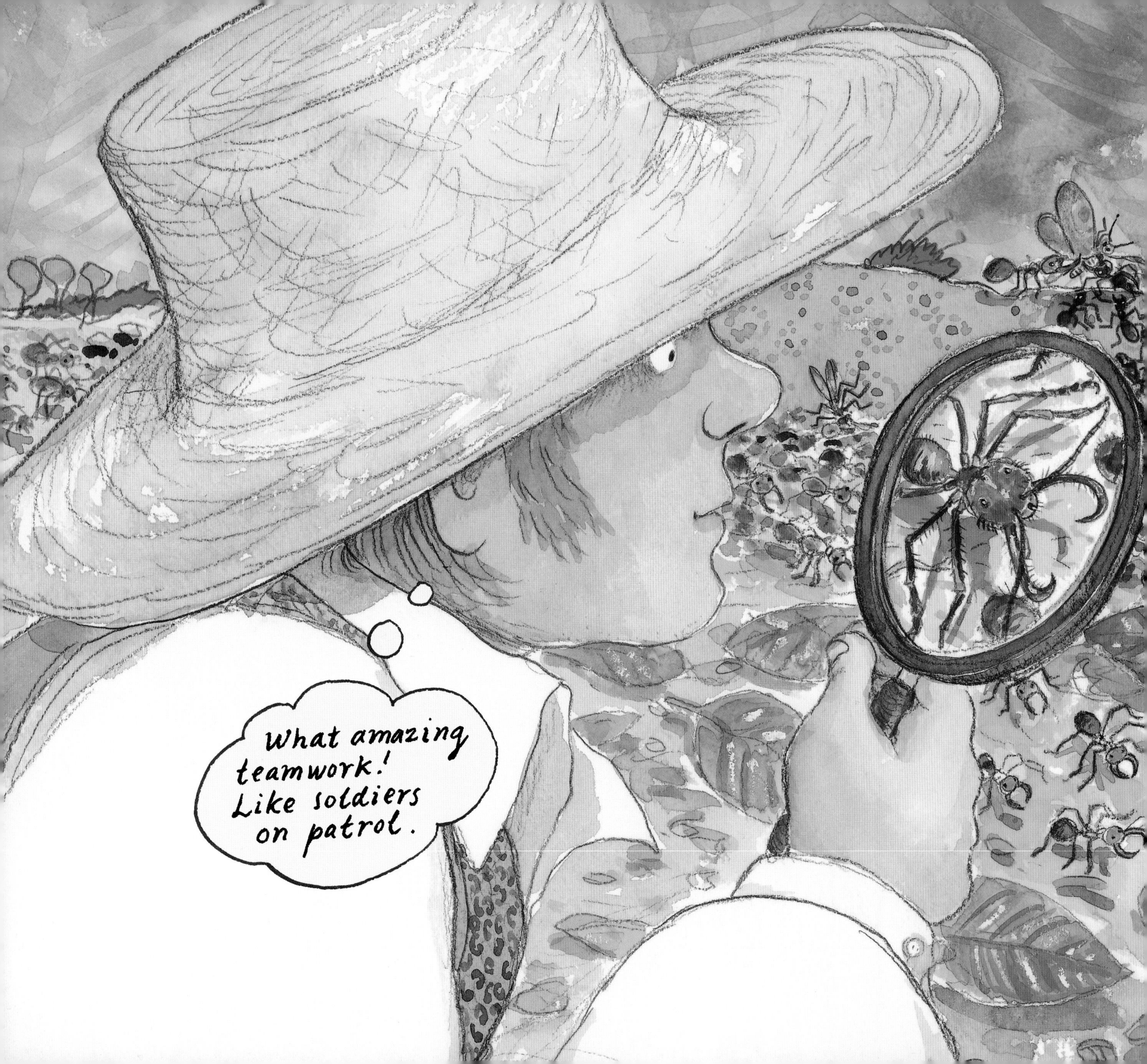
What amazing teamwork! Like soldiers on patrol.

Soldier Ants

A person on first entering a tropical forest is astonished at the labour of ants; well-beaten paths lead in every direction. One day my attention was drawn to many insects and some lizards rushing across a bare piece of ground. A little way behind, every stalk and leaf was blackened by ants. The swarm divided itself and descended an old wall. By this means they surrounded many insects; the efforts the poor little creatures made to extricate themselves from such a death were wonderful.

Penguins breed on land but spend the rest of their life at sea – they make strange grunting cries.

St Elmo's Fire   July 1832

We saw a great shoal of porpoises many hundreds in number. When the ship was running nine knots (17 km/h) these animals could cross and re-cross the bows with the greatest ease. On one dark night we were surrounded by seals and penguins which made such strange noises that the officer on watch reported he could hear cattle bellowing on shore! On the second night we witnessed a splendid scene of natural fireworks . . . the masthead and yardarm shone with St Elmo's fire . . .

All hands on deck! Look at the St Elmo's fire, FitzRoy!

Darwin discovered a new species of dolphin and named it 'FitzRoy's dolphin' to honour the *Beagle*'s commander.

Plants and animals had to be collected and preserved for the long journey to England. FitzRoy found Darwin an assistant, a young sailor called Syms Covington.

FitzRoy and Darwin began to disagree about the truth of Bible stories like the Creation and Noah's Ark.

Punta Alta Fossils *October 1832*

I have been wonderfully lucky with fossil bones. The remains at Punta Alta were embedded in gravel and reddish mud. The great size of the bones of the megatheroid animals including the megatherium, megalonyx and mylodon is truly wonderful. The teeth indicate that these animals lived on vegetable food. Their ponderous forms and great curved claws seem little adapted for locomotion. We started by moonlight and arrived by sunrise. I stayed here the greater part of the day, searching for fossil bones.

Darwin noticed that some of the fossils he found shared similar features such as claws, teeth and armoured skin with smaller living creatures of the pampas. . .

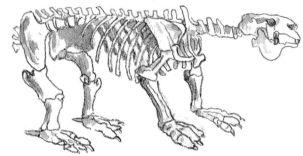

. . . like the pink fairy armadillos and six banded armadillos he saw and ate.

The Argentine Pampas   *August 1833*

My dress was that of the country: poncho, boots, large spurs and straw hat. A brace of pistols completed my appearance. In the morning we caught an armadillo, which, although a most excellent dish when roasted in its shell, did not make a very substantial breakfast.

The armadillos resemble the fossils I found!

Although much smaller.

It's armadillo for breakfast Mr Darwin.

Si Signor!

Darwin travelled with the gauchos – the cowboys of the pampas – and envied their wild freedom.

FitzRoy named Mount Darwin to celebrate his friend's 25th birthday. The fossil sea shells Darwin found proved that the seabed had gradually, over time, been pushed up to form mountains.

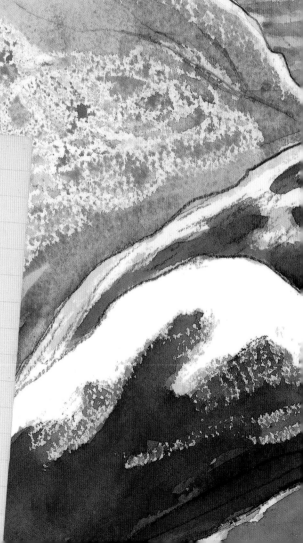

Andes - August 1834

It is wonderful to find shells which were once crawling on the bottom of the sea, now standing nearly 14,000 feet (4270 m) above its level. These shells are embedded in a reddish-black vegetable mould. I was much surprised to find under the microscope that this vegetable mould is really marine mud. We ascended to a great height, but becoming involved in the snow drifts had some difficulty in returning.

Earthquakes can trigger monster waves called tidal waves or tsunamis.

It's an Earthquake, Covington!

Run!

Look! The land has risen...

So this is how mountains are made!

Living seashells had been left high and dry by the earthquake, proving that land could be raised 'slowly and by little starts'.

Chile Earthquake February 1835

The earth, the very emblem of solidity, has moved beneath our feet like a thin crust over a fluid. Shortly after the shock a great wave was seen from the distance of three or four miles (five or six km), approaching with a smooth outline; but along the shore it tore up cottages and trees as it swept onwards with irresistible force. At the head of the bay it broke in a fearful line of white breakers. A cannon, four tons in weight, was moved 15 feet (4.5 m) inwards and a schooner was left in the midst of the ruins 200 yards (180 m) from the beach. The most remarkable effect of this earthquake was the permanent elevation of the land.

Darwin saw that when danger threatened, the marine iguanas returned to land. This proved they were originally land lubbers that had evolved into sea-going animals.

Galapagos Islands Iguanas *September 1835*

One is astonished at the amount of creative force displayed on the small, barren and rocky islands. A remarkable lizard, confined to this archipelago, is common and lives on the rocky beaches. It is a hideous-looking creature, of a dirty black colour, stupid and sluggish in its movements. On the island of Albemarle they seem to grow to a greater size than elsewhere. Their tails are flattened sideways and all feet are partially webbed. The nature of this lizard's food, as well as the structure of the tail and feet, absolutely prove its aquatic habits.

Later, back in England, John Gould explained to Darwin that the birds collected from the Galapagos Islands included a group of finches never described before. All had different beaks, each adapted to tackle the sort of food available on their island.

Darwin and Covington collected as much as they could carry.

Why do tortoises on different islands have different shaped shells?

Galapagos Tortoises   September–October 1835

The natural history of these islands is eminently curious and well deserves attention. The day was glowing hot; but I was well paid by two large tortoises, each of which must have weighed at least 200 pounds (90 kg). These animals are found, I believe, on all the islands of the archipelago. They prefer the high damp parts. Captain Porter has described those from Charles Island as having their shells turned up at the front like a saddle, whilst the tortoises from James Island are rounder, blacker and have a better taste when cooked. It is said that the ship's company of one frigate brought down, in one day, 200 tortoises to the beach.

Australia   *January 1836*

A large tribe of aborigines called the White Cockatoo Men were persuaded to hold a great dancing party. As soon as it grew dark, fires were lighted and the men painted themselves white in spots and lines. The dancing consisted in their running sideways or in Indian file and stamping the ground accompanied by a kind of grunt. There was one called the Emu Dance . . . In another dance one man imitated a kangaroo while a second crawled up and pretended to spear him. After the dancing, boiled rice and sugar was distributed to the delight of all. After several delays from clouded weather we set sail. Farewell Australia!

These ancient customs must date back to the dawn of mankind!

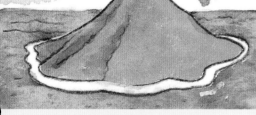

Corals need shallow water and sunlight to live.

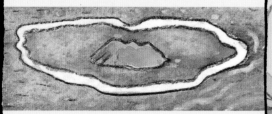

As an island sinks, the coral dies but new layers grow piggyback on the old.

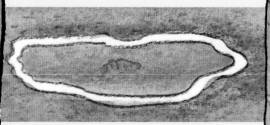

Over time their skeletons form huge reefs – important wildlife habitats. The calm water inside the reef is called a lagoon.

How can these beautiful but tiny coral life forms grow to form huge reefs?

Cocos Islands Coral Lagoon *March 1836*

As a white cloud gives a pleasing contrast with an azure sky, so, in the lagoon, bands of coral darken the emerald green water. The water being unusually smooth, I waded as far as the living mound of coral. Two species of fish, which are common here, exclusively feed on the coral, grazing with their strong bony jaws on the top of the coral branches. Both are coloured a splendid bluish-green. I opened the intestines of several and found them distended with yellowish sandy mud.

Home to England

We made for the shores of England and at Falmouth I left the *Beagle,* having lived on board nearly five years. I settled in lodgings at Cambridge where all my collections were under the care of Henslow. I began preparing my journal of travels. In 1837 I took lodgings in London and remained there for two years. During those two years I was led to think much about religion . . .

Most interesting!

In England Darwin showed his collections to experts like the ornithologist John Gould and the botanist Joseph Hooker.

Darwin married his cousin Emma Wedgwood. He quickly became a famous scientist but it took 20 years before he was ready to publish his theories about the origins of life on earth.

A Visit to the Zoo   1858

Let man visit the orang-utan in captivity and see its intelligence . . . Man in his arrogance thinks himself a great work; more humble, and I believe true, to consider ourselves created from animals.

By cross breeding pigeons using artificial selection, Darwin showed how wild animals evolved by natural selection. Darwin discussed his ideas with scientists like Thomas Huxley and Asa Gray, a professor at Harvard University in the USA.

The Oxford Evolution Debate 1860

When Darwin read about Alfred Russel Wallace's discoveries he realised he had to publish his own ideas or lose all the credit.

Mr Darwin is a genius!

On the Origin of Species was published in 1859 and explained Darwin's 'theory of evolution by natural selection'. It argued against divine creation.

Dear Huxley,

I had a letter from Hooker giving me some account of the battles which have raged about *Origin of Species* at Oxford. He tells me you fought nobly and that you answered the Bishop of Oxford capitally. I honour your pluck! I would sooner have died than as tried to answer the Bishop in such an assembly.

Believe in God not man!

I think I'm going to faint!

Sit down sir!

Booo!

...was it your grandmother or grandfather that was descended from an ape, Huxley?
I wonder how Huxley will answer the bishop?
Huxley is not called Darwin's bulldog for nothing!
Rather an ape than a man who uses his talents to cover up the truth!
Why isn't Darwin here?
He's not feeling well.
That's FitzRoy with the Bible
20 years have passed yet FitzRoy's still angry that Darwin hasn't given the crew of the Beagle more credit!

Goodness me!

Life on Earth, explained Darwin, had evolved over time from primitive beginnings. This shook both the scientific world and the Church!

Origin of Species

When on board HMS *Beagle* as naturalist, I was much struck with certain facts . . . These facts seemed to me to throw some light on the origin of species. It seems to me that man is descended from a hairy, tailed quadruped, probably arboreal in its habits.

FOR EXAMPLE:

OVER CENTURIES, THE PEPPERED MOTH TURNED FROM WHITE TO **BLACK** TO BLEND IN WITH TREES BLACKENED BY CHIMNEY SMOKE.

PALE   DARK

OVER THOUSANDS OF YEARS, DOGS CHANGED THEIR SHAPE AS HUMANS, USING 'ARTIFICIAL SELECTION,' BRED THEM TO SQUEEZE DOWN FOX-HOLES, CHASE RABBITS OR HERD SHEEP... NOW THERE ARE DOGS OF ALL SHAPES AND SIZES.

OVER BILLIONS OF YEARS, SIMPLE LIFE FORMS GROWING IN THE SEA HAVE SLOWLY EVOLVED INTO EVERY LIVING THING ON EARTH!

It's how one type of ape evolved over time into you and me!

This is how Natural Selection works!

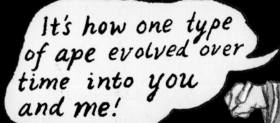

Glossary

Aborigines
The word used in Darwin's time for the native inhabitants of Australia.

Artificial selection
Selection by humans of animals with desirable characteristics for breeding.

Bishop
An important official of the Christian church.

Creationism
The belief that the Biblical story of creation is true in every detail. Some creationists argue against Darwin's discoveries even today.

Evolution
The theory that all species have developed from earlier forms of life on earth.

Extinction
The process of a species of living thing dying out completely.

Evolve
To develop gradually over a period of time.

Fossil
Remains of an animal, or an impression of an animal or plant from ancient times preserved as rock.

Geologist
Scientist who studies geology, Earth's history as told by its landscape, rocks and minerals.

Mate
An animal's breeding partner. Can also mean 'to make babies'.

Megatheroid
A family of extinct ground sloths whose huge fossil bones reminded Darwin of smaller creatures alive today such as anteaters, tree sloths and armadillos.

Natural selection
The process in which animals best suited to survive in particular environments pass on their skills to their young. Over long periods of time this can lead to changes in size, colour, pattern and body structure.

Parasite
A plant or animal that lives on or in another.

St Elmo's Fire
Luminous electricity that can appear, during storms, on ships' masts or church spires.

Taxidermy
The skill of preserving and stuffing animal skins so they appear lifelike.

Biographies

Covington
A young sailor who shot and collected many of Darwin's specimens during the voyage.

FitzRoy – commander of HMS *Beagle*
He invited Darwin to be his companion-naturalist. FitzRoy's leadership kept the crew safe on a voyage that was as dangerous as a mission to Mars would be today. Later with his experience of predicting weather he became 'father of the Met Office' and gave us the 'weather forecast'. FitzRoy and Darwin eventually fell out over creationism and because FitzRoy felt that the crew of the *Beagle* deserved more credit. But Darwin described FitzRoy as 'generous to a fault, bold, determined, energetic and a friend.'

Wallace
Alfred Russel Wallace was a scientist who also travelled the world. He had similar ideas to Darwin about evolution and it was his letter to Darwin explaining his theories that pushed Darwin to publish. First they published a joint paper and then Darwin published his book *On the Origin of Species*.

Voyage of the *Beagle*

HMS *Beagle* had many other adventures we didn't have room to tell you about in this book. FitzRoy had taken three natives of Tierra del Fuego to England on a previous expedition. Hoping to introduce Christianity and 'civilisation' to their homeland he had educated them at his own expense. But when the *Beagle* returned them to their homeland things didn't go as FitzRoy hoped; they returned to their own way of life . . . In South America Darwin saw slavery which he said 'made his blood boil'. He also witnessed the slaughter of the native 'indians' by the Argentinian dictator General Rosas.

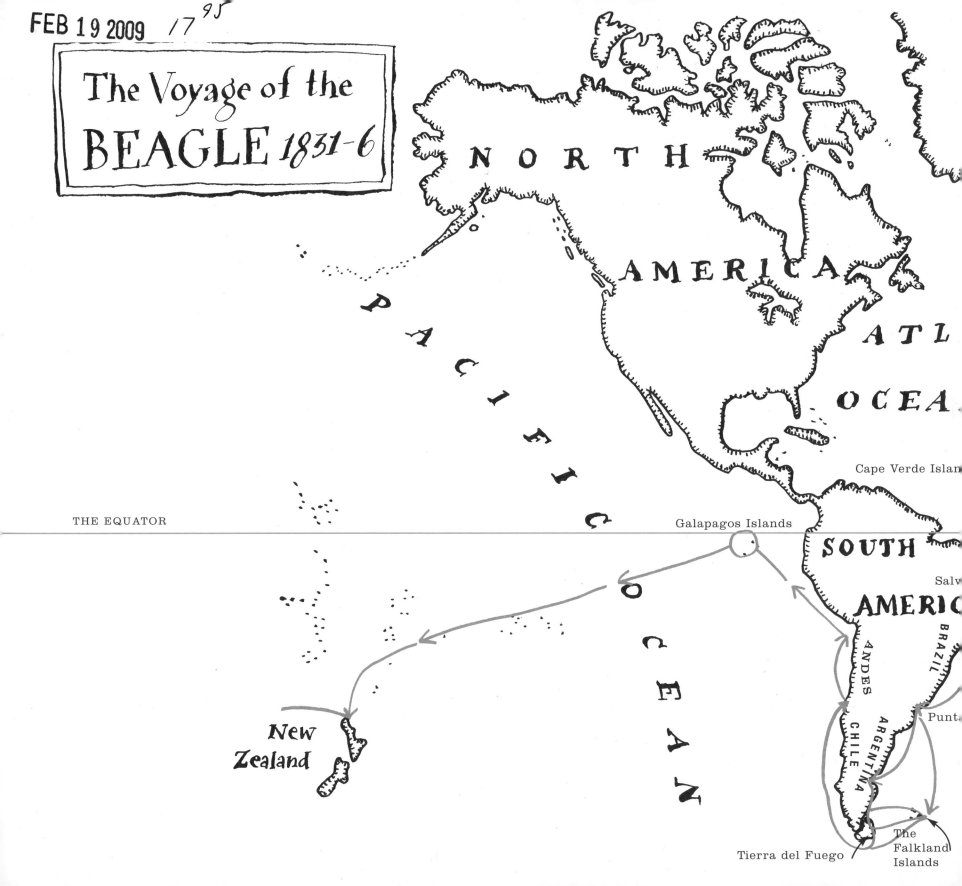

The Voyage of the
BEAGLE 1831-6

N O R T H

A M E R I C A

ATL

OCEA

PACIFIC

Cape Verde Islan

THE EQUATOR

Galapagos Islands

SOUTH

Salv

AMERIC

BRAZIL

O C E A N

ANDES

CHILE

ARGENTINA

Punta

New
Zealand

Tierra del Fuego

The
Falkland
Islands